A ROOKIE BIOGRAPHY

RUDYARD KIPLING

Author of the Jungle Books

By Carol Greene

CHILDRENS PRESS ®
CHICAGO

Rudyard Kipling (1865-1936)

Library of Congress Cataloging-in-Publication Data

Greene, Carol.
    Rudyard Kipling : author of the Jungle books / by Carol Greene.
      p. cm. — (A Rookie biography)
    ISBN 0-516-04266-1
    1. Kipling, Rudyard, 1865-1936—Biography—Juvenile literature.
  2. Authors, English—19th century—Biography—Juvenile literature.
  3. Authors, English—20th century—Biography—Juvenile literature.
  [1. Kipling, Rudyard, 1865-1936. 2. Authors, English.] I. Title. II. Series:
  Greene, Carol. Rookie biography.
  PR4856.G65   1994
  828′.809—dc20
  [B]   94-11940
                                              CIP
                                              AC

Rudyard Kipling
was a real person.
He was born in 1865.
He died in 1936.
Kipling wrote many
great stories and poems.
Some were for children.
This is his story.

TABLE OF CONTENTS

Rudyard Kipling
was born in
Bombay, India.
Many poor
people struggled
to make a
living in the
crowded city.

Chapter 1

India and England

Bombay, India, was a
beautiful city—
and a terrible city.
Garden smells and temple bells,
deadly sickness and beggars' cries
all mixed together there.

Rudyard Kipling's parents came
to Bombay from England
before Rudyard was born.
His father started an art school.
So to Rudyard, Bombay
was home and he loved it.

Sometimes Rudyard played
at his father's school.
But he and his little sister Trix
spent most of their time with
the family's Indian servants.

Servants took them for walks
and cared for Rudyard's pony.
They told them stories and
made them toys from oranges.

Soon Rudyard could speak
the servants' language.
Sometimes he even forgot to
speak English to his parents.

At night, Rudyard lay in bed
and listened to the wind
blow through the palm leaves.
Tree frogs sang him to sleep
and all was well.

Families working on boats in an Indian lake

But everything changed when
Rudyard was five and a half
and Trix was almost three.

English children did not do well
in the hot Indian summers.
So their parents took them
back to England.

The Kiplings took
Rudyard and Trix
to live with
the Holloway family.
Then they went back to India.

"You must call us Aunty Rosa and
Uncle Harry," said the Holloways.
They had a son named Harry too.
Their house was small and ugly
and they would not give
the children enough to eat.

Rudyard and Trix had to
spend a lot of time in
a basement room that
smelled like mushrooms.
It was so cold that they got
sores called chilblains.

Aunty Rosa liked Trix.
But she didn't like Rudyard.
She scolded him and beat him.

Young Harry beat Rudyard too.
He said cruel things to Trix
and pinched her till she had
bruises all over her arms.
Rudyard called him Devil-Boy.

Uncle Harry was not so bad.
But after a while, he died.

The Kipling children lived with
the Holloways for five years.
During this time, they never
saw their parents.
But they did learn to read.

**Rudyard Kipling
as a boy**

Rudyard loved reading.
It made him feel as if
he were someplace else.
But then his eyes got bad.
He couldn't read at all.
He could hardly see.

At last Mrs. Kipling came
for her children and
the terrible years were over.

Chapter 2

Growing Up

Mrs. Kipling felt bad
when she learned what
her children had gone through.
So she lived with them
in a little farmhouse
next to a forest.

Now Rudyard and Trix
could run free.
They picked flowers,
rode horses, milked cows,
and played with the barn cats.

Sometimes a Gypsy man
took them for donkey rides
deep into the forest.

Sometimes they played
in a windmill.
Rudyard said it was full of
"lovely rumbling floury places."

Rudyard got glasses so
he could see and read again.
Then it was time for him
to go away to school.

He went to a boys' school,
the United Services College.
It sat by the shore in a town
called Westward Ho!, England.

Rudyard (in glasses) on a return visit to the United Services College

Those four years at school
were good for Rudyard.
He had two fine teachers
and made some good friends.
He edited the school paper.
He wrote stories and poems.

When Rudyard was almost 17,
he finished school.
Then he went to work for
a newspaper in India.
It was a tough job,
but he learned a lot.

Rudyard liked to watch
all sorts of people.
He listened to their stories
and to how they spoke.
He also liked to visit
strange and different places.

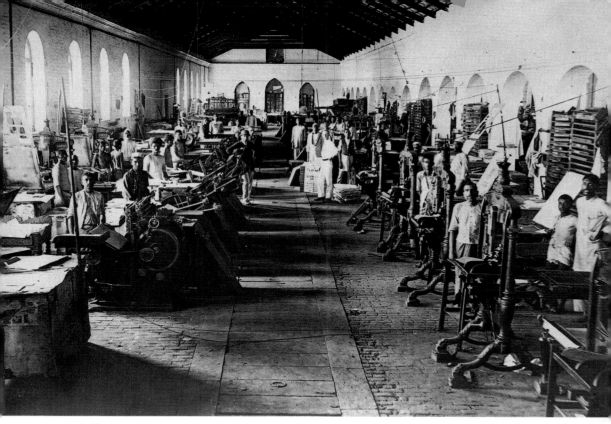

Printers at work at the Allahabad Pioneer Press (above).
Many of Kipling's early works were printed there. Kipling
wrote some of his most famous stories in the Blue Room
(below) at Belvedere House in Allahabad, India.

Then Rudyard put
what he saw and heard
into stories and poems.
He couldn't stop writing.

Soon Rudyard's first little
book of poems came out.
It made him famous
all over India.

A portrait
of the
young writer

Bond Street, London, looked like this in the 1890s.

As time went by, Rudyard
decided he didn't want to
work for newspapers anymore.
He wanted to write full-time.
So in 1889, he moved
to London, England.

Kipling loved the
lively city of
London. The
Strand (right) was
a busy street
full of traffic
and noise. These
women (bottom)
sold fresh-cut
flowers to passersby.

Chapter 3

A Family for Rudyard

People in London
already knew and liked
Rudyard's stories and poems.
They wanted more.
Soon he had plenty of work.

**Kipling lived in this house
in Villiers Street, London.**

But Rudyard
often felt lonely.
He needed a family.
He also needed
someone to
take care of
practical things,
such as money.
Rudyard was
not practical.

Then he made friends with
an American, Wolcott Balestier,
and his sister, Carrie.
When Wolcott died, Rudyard
and Carrie became very close.
In 1892, they got married.

The young Kiplings thought
they would start their new life
with a trip around the world.
But they got only
as far as Japan.

Then the bank where Rudyard
kept his money failed.
The Kiplings were broke.
So they went to Carrie's
family home in Vermont.

The Kiplings lived for a while in Brattleboro, Vermont.

Kipling (center) next to a horse-drawn sled in Brattleboro, 1893

Rudyard loved Vermont.
He walked in the woods
and talked to the farmers.
He watched the seasons change.
Soon he and Carrie began
to build their own home.

Then their first child,
Josephine, was born.
Later, the Kiplings had two
more children, Elsie and John.
But Josephine would always
be special to Rudyard.

Kipling in his study at his Vermont home

At last he had a home
and a family.

And Carrie took care of
the practical things.
Rudyard was a happy man.

27

This illustration from the *Jungle Book* shows Mowgli with
the wolf pack. Bagheera the panther is standing by.

Chapter 4

Stories for Children

Rudyard wrote many stories
in his Vermont home.
Some of the best ones
are in the *Jungle Books.*

These stories tell about
Mowgli, a human baby
who was raised by
a pack of wolves
in the Indian jungle.

Mowgli with
his friends,
Baloo the bear
and Bagheera
the panther

Many jungle animals
help Mowgli grow up:
Baloo the bear,
Bagheera the panther,
Kaa the python,
and others.

Rudyard also wrote
Captains Courageous.
It's about a rich boy
who became a man by
working on a fishing boat.

An illustration from *Captains Courageous*

The Kiplings lived in this country house in England.

In 1896, the Kiplings
moved back to England.
There Rudyard wrote
more books for children.

This illustration from *Stalky and Co.* shows Stalky (second from right) and his friends punishing two bullies (tied up at left).

He got ideas for one,
Stalky and Co.,
from his own school days.

In 1899, the Kiplings
visited New York.
All at once, Rudyard
became very sick.
So did Josephine.

Rudyard got well again, but Josephine died. Rudyard never got over that. He missed his little girl for the rest of his life.

A painting of Kipling at work

In 1900, the Kiplings began to spend their winters in South Africa. There Rudyard told Elsie and John the *Just So Stories*. The children loved them.

The *Just So Stories* tell about "The Elephant's Child" and "the great grey-green greasy Limpopo River."

They tell about "The Cat That Walked by Himself" and "How the Camel Got His Hump." There are two stories and some poems about Josephine too.

This drawing is from "How the Camel Got His Hump."

Rudyard also drew pictures
to go with the stories.
They were very good and
Rudyard was proud of them.

Rudyard didn't write
his book *Kim* for children.
But Kim is a boy spy
and many children like
the book anyway.

Rudyard's last
two books
for children are
Puck of Pook's Hill
and *Rewards and
Fairies*. They tell
about the history
of England and
magical stories.

A picture from
the story
"The Joyous
Venture"

Kipling (second from right) talks at a meeting in London in 1915. The people at the meeting were trying to get young men to join the army.

Rewards and Fairies came out in 1910. After that, Rudyard wrote only for adults, and many of the things he wrote were sad.

Chapter 5

Sad, Angry Years

Rudyard had always liked to learn about war. He liked to be with soldiers and sailors. He wrote a lot about war too.

Rudyard knew that
World War I was coming
before other people did.
He was proud when his son
John wanted to fight.

But early in the war
young John was killed.
That almost broke
Rudyard's heart.

Kipling on his sixty-fifth birthday

Rudyard also had strong
ideas about how
governments should work.
He got very angry when
people didn't agree with him.

Rudyard's last years
were not happy ones.
Sores called ulcers
gave him a lot of pain.
Getting angry so often
wasn't good for him either.

Carrie was often sick too.
But she did all she
could for Rudyard.
And she still took care
of the practical things.

Rudyard and Carrie Kipling in 1928

Rudyard Kipling (left) meets with King George V of Great Britain in 1922.

The cartoon (inset) shows Kipling working in India
while the animals he wrote about look on.

Rudyard Kipling died
in London in 1936.
He left behind many
people who loved him—
and many who didn't.

But he also left behind
great stories and poems,
including many for children.

Important Dates

1865   December 30—Born in Bombay, India, to Alice and Lockwood Kipling

1871   Began stay with Holloway family at Southsea, England

1878   Began studies at United Services College, Westward Ho!, England

1882   Began work at *The Civil and Military Gazette*, Lahore, India

1889   Moved to London, England

1892   Married Caroline (Carrie) Balestier
Moved to Brattleboro, Vermont

1894   The *Jungle Book* published

1895   The *Second Jungle Book* published

1896   Returned to England

1902   The *Just So Stories* published

1907   Received Nobel Prize

1936   January 18—Died in London, England

INDEX

Page numbers in boldface type indicate illustrations.

ABOUT THE AUTHOR

Carol Greene has degrees in English literature and musicology. She has worked
in international exchange programs, as an editor, and as a teacher of writing.
She now lives in Webster Groves, Missouri, and writes full-time. She has
published more than 100 books, including those in the Childrens Press Rookie
Biographies series.